First World War
and Army of Occupation
War Diary
France, Belgium and Germany

61 DIVISION
Headquarters, Branches and Services
1 July 1918 - 15 July 1918

WO95/3041/1

The Naval & Military Press Ltd
www.nmarchive.com
Published in association with The National Archives

Published by

The Naval & Military Press Ltd

Unit 10 Ridgewood Industrial Park,

Uckfield, East Sussex,

TN22 5QE England

Tel: +44 (0) 1825 749494

www.naval-military-press.com

www.nmarchive.com

This diary has been reprinted in facsimile from the original. Any imperfections are inevitably reproduced and the quality may fall short of modern type and cartographic standards.

© **Crown Copyright**
Images reproduced by permission of The National Archives, London, England, 2015.

Contents

Document type	Place/Title	Date From	Date To
Heading	WO95/3041/1		
Heading	61st Division CRE 1918 Jly-1919Jly		
Heading	War Diary of Hd Qrs 61st (S.M) Div RE For The Month of July 1918		
War Diary	P.1.a.4.5.	01/07/1918	02/07/1918
War Diary	0.6.b.8.4.	02/07/1918	11/07/1918
War Diary	M.5.c.7.3. Ham	12/07/1918	15/07/1918

WO 95/30411

61ST DIVISION

C. R. E.

~~JAN 1918 - JLY 1919~~

1918 JLY — 1919 JLY

Confidential

Vol 27

WAR DIARY
OF
HQrs. 61st (S.M.) Div R.E
FOR THE MONTH OF
JULY 1918

Vol XXVI

Army Form C. 2118.

WAR DIARY
or
INTELLIGENCE SUMMARY

(Erase heading not required.)

HEADQUARTERS.
61st. DIV. ROYAL ENGINEERS.
Vol. XXVII   Page 1.

Instructions regarding War Diaries and Intelligence Summaries are contained in F.S. Regs., Part II. and the Staff Manual respectively. Title pages will be prepared in manuscript.

Place	Date	Hour	Summary of Events and Information	Remarks and references to Appendices
P.1.a.4.5.	JULY. 1918. Sheet 36a. 1/40000 FRANCE.			
	1st.		Nominal Roll of Unit	
		10.30 am.	Received advice that 1 section 439 Field Co (74th. Divn) will move to ST. VENANT asylum for work under 61st. Division. G.S.O.1. telephoned to say that the XI Corps disapproves of move of D.H.Q and 476 Field Co should discontinue building the new camp. Telephoned "Q" who said that work should be stopped pending return of G.O.C. who is out and "Q" will send orders to 476 Field Co to stop work. C.R.E. visited forward area with O's. C. 478 and 479 Field Cos General GRANT, C.E. Fifth Army called and informed us that we are in Fifth Army from today.	Appx 4.
0.6.b.8.4.	2nd		R.E. Headquarters moved to late H.Q. of 476 Field Co. Captain J.K. RENNIE (R.A.M.C) rejoined R.E.H.Q from hospital. Captain HUMPHREYS assumed Command of 479 Field Co vice Major O.S. DAVIES, D.S.O. C.R.E. visited forward area. During the evening C.R.E. and Adjutant developed P.U.O - Most of our officers are down with it now.	
	3rd.		30 men from Labour Corps were attached to 478 Field Co for cutting crops in forward area. Lieut-Colonel G.E.J. DURNFORD, D.S.O (C.R.E) went to hospital with P.U.O. and Major M. WHITWILL, D.S.O., M.C. assumed temporary command of Divisional R.E.	
	4th.		Issued Notes on Conference held today. 30 men of Labour Corps rejoined their unit as a result of their lodging objection to working in the forward area.	Appx 3.

Army Form C. 2118.

WAR DIARY
or
INTELLIGENCE SUMMARY.
(Erase heading not required.)

HEADQUARTERS.
61st. DIVNL. ROYAL ENGINEERS.

Vol XXVII

Page 2.

Instructions regarding War Diaries and Intelligence Summaries are contained in F.S. Regs., Part II. and the Staff Manual respectively. Title pages will be prepared in manuscript.

JULY. 1918.

Place	Date	Hour	Summary of Events and Information	Remarks and references to Appendices
FRANCE. Sht. 36a. 1/40000				
O.6.b.8.4.	4.	1 pm.	Received 61st. Divisional Order 174 re relief of 183 Brigade by 184 Brigade, and this was cancelled later owing to Divisional relief which is shortly to take place. G.S.O.1. called.	
	5th			
	6th.		Received 184 Brigade Order 190 re relief of 183 Brigade 9/10th, but this was cancelled later owing to Divisional Relief Issued Divisional R.E. Defence Scheme and Appendices	Appx 5
	7th.	1 pm. 2.45pm	Received 183 Brigade Order 224 re relief by 184 Brigade, and this was cancelled owing to relief Received 183 Brigade Order 223 re earlier raid by East Lancs at 11 p.m. Received report on action of 61st. Division April 10th-30th 1918 (61 Div G.C. 40/5)	
	8th.	pm 6.30 7 pm.	C.E. XI Corps called and stated that relief of 61 by 74 Divn will commence on 10th. inst. C.R.E. 74 Division called and discussed relief. Received 61 Div Order 175 warning re relief of Division Issued Warning order 24/2/1 to Companies re relief of Division by 74 Division Issued Notes on Conference held 5 p.m. today Lce/Corporal E.G. ANGELL (our draughtsman) went to hospital with P.U.O.	Appx 2 Appx 3

Army Form C. 2118.

WAR DIARY
or
INTELLIGENCE SUMMARY

(Erase heading not required.)

HEADQUARTERS.
61st. DIV. ROYAL ENGINEERS.
Vol. XXVII

Page 3

Place	Date	Hour	Summary of Events and Information	Remarks and references to Appendices
O.6.b.8.4.	JULY 1918. FRANCE. Sht. 36a. 1/40000.			
	9th.	am 8.30	Received 61 Div Order 176 re relief of 61 Div by 74 Div 10th-14th inst Issued R.E. Order 103 re relief of 61 Div R.E by 74 Div R.E. Received 74 Div Order 22 re relief of 61 Div R.E. Received 183 Brigade Order 225 re Div. Relief Received A.D.M.S. order re Medical Arrangements on relief Adjutant went to HAM via "Q" office to arrange for the billeting of the whole Divisional R.E in that village, and called in on the way back at 476 Field Co to arrange for that Company to move to HAM tomorrow morning. Lieut-Colonel G.E.J. DURNFORD, D.S.O. rejoined from hospital and resumed command of Div. R.E Captain J.K. RENNIE (R.A.M.C) proceeded on one months special leave and was relieved by Captain TOBIAS (R.A.M.C)	Appx 2
	10th		G.S.O.1. called. XI Corps maintains that the Divisional R.E must administer the supply of all R.E. stores required by the Division when in the back area training. This attitude was strongly contested and ultimately Divisional Headquarters took the matter up with the result that all requirements of units will be attended to by area commandants.	
	11th		Issued orders for move of R.E.H.Qrs tomorrow to HAM. C.R.E. 74 Division called and was taken round the line by Major WHITWILL, D.S.O, M.C. (478 Field Co). He brought his stores officers up and he is to remain with us until the relief	Appx 2

Army Form C. 2118.

WAR DIARY
or
INTELLIGENCE SUMMARY
(Erase heading not required.)

HEADQUARTERS.
61st. DIVN. ROYAL ENGINEERS.
Vol. XXVII.   Page 4

Place	Date	Hour	Summary of Events and Information	Remarks and references to Appendices
~~Oxford~~ M.5.c.7.3. HAM	JULY 1918. 12th		FRANCE. Sht. 36a. 1/40000 R.E. Headquarters moved to HAM after handing over to C.R.E. 74th. Division. Issued Routine Orders 85 - 90 G.O.C. called at R.E.H.Qrs HAM.	Appx 2 Appx 1
	13th.		Issued Routine Orders 95 - 98 Companies spent the day improving their billets and preparing for vigorous training to commence on MONDAY.	Appx 1
	14th.	9.30am	Church Parade. Issued Notes on Conference held at 11 a.m. today. Corporal F.L. PENNY proceeded on leave to U.K. Received notification that Division (less 183 Brigade) is in G.H.Q. Reserve at 24 hours notice and 183 Brigade at 8 hours notice. C.R.E. reconnoitred various training grounds and rifle ranges.	Appx 3
	15th		Issued Routine Orders 96 and 97 re training Received 61 Div Order 177- 184 Brigade to exchange billeting accomodation with 183 Brigade. -the former will now be at 8 hours notice	Appx 1

www.ingramcontent.com/pod-product-compliance
Lightning Source LLC
Chambersburg PA
CBHW081517160426
43193CB00014B/2716